seventeen

real girls, real-life stories

TRUE
L♥VE

real girls, real-life stories

TRUE

LVE

YA
306.73
S 497

From the Editors of *Seventeen* Magazine

Hearst Books
A Division of Sterling Publishing Co., Inc.
New York

These stories are reprinted from *Seventeen* magazine 2003 to 2006.

Book design by Kelly Roberts

Cover photo: Todd Marshard

Library of Congress Cataloging-in-Publication Data

Seventeen real girls, real-life stories : true love / from the editors of
Seventeen Magazine.

    p. cm.

 Includes index.

 ISBN-13: 978-1-58816-629-6 (alk. paper)

 ISBN-10: 1-58816-629-5 (alk. paper)

 1. Dating (Social customs)—Case studies—Juvenile literature.
2. Interpersonal relations in adolescence—Case studies—Juvenile
literature. 3. Love—Case studies—Juvenile literature. 4. Teenagers—
United States—Case studies—Juvenile literature. I. Seventeen.

 HQ801.A2S48 2007

 306.730835—dc22

                      2006025583

10 9 8 7 6 5 4 3 2 1

Published by Hearst Books
A Division of Sterling Publishing Co., Inc.
387 Park Avenue South, New York, NY 10016

Seventeen and Hearst Books are trademarks of
Hearst Communications, Inc.

www.seventeen.com

For information about custom editions, special sales, premium and
corporate purchases, please contact Sterling Special Sales
Department at 800-805-5489 or specialsales@sterlingpub.com.

Distributed in Canada by Sterling Publishing
c/o Canadian Manda Group, 165 Dufferin Street
Toronto, Ontario, Canada M6K 3H6

Distributed in Australia by Capricorn Link (Australia) Pty. Ltd.
P.O. Box 704, Windsor, NSW 2756 Australia

Printed in United States

Sterling ISBN 13: 978-1-58816-629-6
       ISBN 10: 1-58816-629-5

contents

foreword

Hey!

Sometimes society paints love out to be a big fairy-tale: As in, once you meet your Prince Charming, you'll fall in love and live happily ever after.

The most important lesson *we've* learned?

Just because a relationship doesn't last forever, doesn't mean it was a failure. Try this: Take a look at your last relationship and figure out what you learned and how you grew. What an amazing gift he gave you, right? Now, let it end on that beautiful note, as opposed to being angry and clawing to stay together.

We hope the stories in this book will inspire you and remind you of another important lesson: Love isn't a destination. It's a journey that can be wonderful and challenging–sometimes both at the same time. Enjoy the journey.

–the Editors of *seventeen*

opposites attract

Do you have a particular "type" of guy that you always go for? Kelly, 21, did—until she realized the benefits of dating someone totally different.

i always went out with the preppy guys—the goody-goody types who wear American Eagle Outfitters and get straight A's. They were the guys that I felt comfortable with—they looked and acted like me. And let's just say that Bobby was not one of those guys.

I IGNORED HIM

In high school, Bobby and I went to the same church, but that's where our similarities ended. He played in a rock band, wasn't into school, and had a three-inch-tall mohawk; I was three years younger, in the *marching* band, and got mostly A's. But he was still kind of cute and funny—and I had fun flirting with him. Even so, when he finally left for college (a full two years after graduating high school), we didn't keep in touch at all.

A year later, I was a freshman at Indiana University. I didn't even remember that Bobby was at IU—until he e-mailed me my first month there and invited me over. I thought it was nice of him to get in touch, so I went. But his house was gross: There was food on the floor and posters of pot leaves plastered on the walls. It freaked me out, so I left after a half hour. And the next time he e-mailed, I didn't even reply.

HE KEPT TRYING

Over the next year or so, I dated my usual smart, preppy guys—but they all ended up being more into school than me. And all that time Bobby kept e-mailing and asking me to hang out when he'd see me on campus. I knew he was being friendly, but you know how you can tell when a guy wants to be *more* than friends? That's how it felt with Bobby. I liked him, but I wasn't interested in him *that* way. So I ignored his invites—I didn't want to encourage him.

> **66** You know how you can tell when a guy wants to be more than friends? **99**

But by the end of my sophomore year, I started to feel bad about brushing Bobby off since he was always so nice, so I invited him to have dinner with me and my roommates. They loved him, and when he left, they were like, "You guys *have* to go out." My gut reaction was, "Are you kidding?!" I mean, we couldn't be more different: He had six tattoos *and* was a total slacker—he took only two classes a semester, when I had five.

I WAS AN IDIOT

After that dinner, my roommates started inviting Bobby over—even when I wasn't there. He'd send me flowers and leave burned CDs for me in my room, but I

still considered us "just good friends." Yet I was
starting to get weirdly jealous when my roommates
spent more time with him than I did. . . .

Even though I didn't want to date Bobby, we *were*
getting closer. We'd have long talks, and I learned so
much about him. I had thought he did drugs but found
out that he was really just overwhelmed with
emotional stuff after his younger sister died. That's also
why he only took two classes at a time. As we spent
more time together, I stopped seeing Bobby as this
rebel type. He wasn't dumb or a slacker—Bobby was a
real thinking and feeling guy.

One night I went with Bobby to hear a band play,
and I watched him joking, smiling, and laughing with
everyone. I suddenly felt like such an idiot! Bobby was
the nicest person I'd ever been around *and* he genuinely
cared about me. So why was I holding back? As soon as
I realized how blind I'd been, I grabbed his hand and
told him I was falling in love with him.

I'M IN LOVE

Bobby and I have been together for over a year now.
Yes, on the outside we look like the kind of couple that
only a reality show would put together. But I love how
we balance each other out on the inside: He's so
easygoing that he gets me to slow down when I take
my work too seriously, and I've helped him focus on
school (he's finally graduating this December!).

I don't know what'll happen to us when we leave
campus, but I'll do anything to make this work.

getting
over him

Kaitlin, 16, was thrilled when she started
dating her first boyfriend—but then he broke her
heart. How do you finally get over the first one?

O n July 4 last year my friend Jen and I went
to a nearby town to meet her cousin and
some of her friends. As a big group of us sat
on blankets and watched the fireworks, I kept staring
at this one guy, Tim. He was talking to everyone and
just seemed so comfortable and confident. During the
night Tim and I made the connection that he lived on
the same street as my grandparents! He asked if we
could exchange phone numbers—I was so excited!

FALLING FAST

By the first week of school, Tim had asked me to be his
girlfriend. Since we lived in different towns, he'd call
me every day after school, but if I wasn't there, he'd
text me "just to say I miss you." We also hung out
whenever we could. On October 3, my 15th birthday,
Tim even gave up a weekend trip with his friends to
come to my party. That night, as we were outside my
house, kissing, he said, "Happy birthday—I love you." It
was the first time anyone had told me that, and I felt

13

amazing. I'd never realized how much I could care about a guy—or how much someone could like me. One Sunday about two months later I called Tim, but he wasn't home. So I IM'd our friend Joe to see if he knew where Tim was. Joe said that he didn't, and then wrote, "You shouldn't care about Tim so much." I began panicking that he knew something I didn't, so I asked him why he said that—but he said I needed to ask Tim. So I immediately called Tim on his cell (thank God he answered) and asked him what Joe meant. At first he was silent, so I asked, "Is there something you don't want me to find out?" He slowly said, "Um, I hooked up with another girl." I was so hurt and furious—and I didn't know if I should hang up and cry, or scream! But Tim didn't give me a chance to do either. Right away he said, "I wasn't thinking—I really love you, Kaitlin. I want to keep going out."

> **66 I didn't know if I should hang up and cry, or scream! 99**

LOSING EVERYTHING

I really loved Tim and couldn't picture life without him. It turned out he'd hooked up just one time with this girl he barely knew, so I forgave him. But then two months later, he began hanging out with this other girl, Morgan, almost every day after school. One night on the phone I told Tim I didn't like it. I expected him to apologize—but instead he got mad at *me* for being clingy! Then *I* got mad at *him* for trying to make *me* feel like the problem. As I tried to get Tim to see things my way, he said, "I don't care anymore—it's over." I was so frustrated that I said, "Fine!"

But reliving everything with my friends the next day at lunch made it sink in that our relationship was actually *over*—and I began to feel depressed and really insecure. I started to panic: How would I get through the weeks without looking forward to our weekends together? I know it sounds pathetic, but even after Tim cheated on me *and* dumped me, I still really wanted to be with him—I kept thinking of how special he used to make me feel. I was so desperate for our old relationship that I called him almost once a day for the next month. But he'd just say, "What do you want me to do, Kaitlin?" I'd even do things like go to the mall after I heard he was there, hoping to "run into" him—but I never did.

MOVING FORWARD

I haven't seen Tim since we broke up 10 months ago, mostly because he hasn't wanted to see me—which used to make me feel bad about myself. But at least not seeing Tim helped me forget him and move on. When you fall in love, you think you can't live without your boyfriend. But sometimes, you have no choice.

the
multi-dater

Jill, 20, wanted to play the field. But can a girl date three guys at the same time and not hurt *any* of them?

C had and I met at a party in March 2001, when I was a sophomore and he was a senior in high school. I was instantly attracted to him—so I was thrilled when he called to ask me out the next day. For two months, we'd hang out a few times a week and have fun. But then I heard rumors that he was seeing another girl. "Are you dating anyone else?" I asked. "Yeah," he said. "I mean, we never said we were going to be exclusive, right?" I played it off like it was no big deal, but I was crushed. I liked him so much that I never even *thought* of dating other people. Now I felt stupid—it seemed like I was more into him than he was into me. So I figured getting serious had been a mistake and decided I should date around too.

NEW BOYS

In late May I noticed a guy who was new to our school. I said hi to him in the hallway, and later that day, he sat next to me in English class and said, "I'm Matt." We started chatting, and I invited him to eat lunch with

17

me. I was really starting to like Matt. We ate lunch together every day over the next two weeks, and I thought he was totally cute. So when he asked me out two weeks later, I happily agreed.

By early June, Matt and I had gone out a few times. I knew he liked me—he'd call a lot just to see how I was doing. It was an ego boost, but I wanted to keep things casual because I still had strong feelings for Chad too.

Then later that month, Carlos, a guy I'd gone to school with since junior high, began talking to me more in class. I'd always thought he had a crush on me, so I wasn't too surprised when he asked me one day, "Do you want to have dinner sometime?" I thought he was funny and sweet, so I figured, Why not? All this attention made me feel beautiful *and* desirable—and the more guys noticed me, the more confident I felt.

Suddenly I was dating three guys at once, and I loved it! None of them officially asked me to be exclusive, and I made a point to avoid that conversation because I didn't want to start a fight or drive them away. Luckily our school was so big they never knew what was going on.

66 All this attention made me feel beautiful and desirable. 99

DISASTROUS DAY

One Saturday in July, I made two dates: to have breakfast with Carlos and to meet up with Matt in the afternoon to go to the local pool. In the morning, Carlos and I had a great time. But later when Matt

and I got to the pool, I couldn't believe my bad luck—
Carlos was there too! I tried to grab Matt and leave,
but Carlos saw us and started walking over. "Are you
guys on a date?" he snapped. "Yeah," Matt said. "I
can't believe you'd do this!" Carlos yelled at me and
stormed off. I was mortified and said to Matt, "We
went out *twice*—we never even kissed!" But Matt
muttered, "Let's talk about this later," and drove me
home. It started to sink in how selfish I was acting.

That night I was in my room when my doorbell
rang—I was so glad to see it was Chad. "I was nearby
and thought I'd say hi," he said. As I was about to let
him in, I saw Matt's car pull into my driveway. My
heart dropped. He got out and saw Chad. "I came to
talk," he said, "but I see you're busy with *another* guy."
As he got back in his car and left, I stood there feeling
ashamed that I'd hurt him *again*. "What's going on?"
Chad asked. I started crying and told him all about
Matt and Carlos. "But I really have feelings for *you*," I
explained. He leaned over, hugged me, and said, "I
don't like that you've been dating other guys. Can we
just see each other?" "Yes," I whispered. But as happy as
I was to have Chad, I felt sick about what I'd done to
Carlos and Matt.

LESSON LEARNED

The next day I called both of them to apologize and
say I'd decided to be with Chad. Neither of them
wanted to stay friends with me. I was so naive to
think I could date a lot of people without breaking
anyone's heart. But now I know that someone always
gets burned.

why i cheated on my girlfriend

Do you ever worry that your guy might cheat? Brendan, 20, explains what made him betray the girl *he* loved.

ver since second grade, I'd been best friends with this girl, Sonya. But the truth is, I had always really liked her as more than a friend. So finally, in 11th grade, I went for it—and kissed her. After that, we became a couple. Since we knew each other so well, things moved really fast—physically *and* emotionally. We became inseparable, and although I'd never been in love before, I *knew* I loved Sonya.

SECOND THOUGHTS

About four months after that first kiss, I began to freak out a little. Even though I was having a great time with Sonya, I'd never been in a serious relationship before, and I started to feel trapped. I mean, Sonya and I got along so well that I thought we might end up getting married. But what if there were even *better* girl out there? How would I *know*?

Everyone knew that Sonya and I were together, but there was still this girl, Becky*, who flirted with me. One day after school, Becky and I were talking when she asked, "Wanna come help me study for math tonight?" I'm *terrible* at math—so I *knew* she was just hitting on me. And I knew I should say no. But I was flattered—and thought this might be my chance to see how it would feel with somebody else.

> **❝What if there were an even *better* girl out there?❞**

That night when I went to Becky's, she was in her cheerleader uniform, which was funny since there hadn't been a game. "Come in, my parents aren't home," she said. So I walked in and sat next to her on the couch. We began talking—but then she suddenly turned to me, swung her legs over mine, leaned in—and kissed me on the lips!

My mind immediately flashed to Sonya. She'd always been there for me, and here I was, blatantly betraying her. Still, I let Becky kiss me. I was just too curious about what it'd be like...and honestly? She was hot! Soon we were making out; she even took off her top. I was definitely into it—until I suddenly realized that we were close to having sex. "Oh, God. I can't," I said panicking. "What?!" Becky asked, fumbling for her clothes. "I'm sorry," I said—and left.

As I drove home, I felt nauseated. I had screwed up, and I kept thinking I was going to lose Sonya over

22

it. The next day at school, when Sonya asked me, "Hey! How was your night?" I felt even worse. She thought I'd been out with friends—and she totally trusted me. I couldn't deal with how badly I felt, so I just said, "Gotta run. See you later!"

THREE'S A CROWD

Later that day, I asked Becky to keep things quiet, and she agreed. But I still worried that Sonya would find out—and I felt *awful* about what I'd done. So for the next two years, I dedicated myself to being a faithful boyfriend to her.

Last fall after I left for college, Sonya and I got into a talk about trust. Finally I decided that it was time to tell her about Becky. She didn't cry—she just said, "Don't tell me details." It seemed like we were moving past it all, but then two months later, she broke up with me: I was devastated. I guess I cheated so I'd know Sonya was the one, but it was so dumb. No one has ever loved me like she did—and I disrespected that.

the romance diet

Losing weight didn't get Miriam, 19, noticed by guys—but *gaining* something did.

When I was in high school, guys never asked me out—they ignored me and always hit on my sister, who's a year older, instead. I'd feel totally rejected, but at the same time I wasn't really surprised. You see, I was about 60 pounds overweight and could never imagine why any guy would think I was cute or want to date me.

FRESH START

Even though I wasn't happy about my appearance, it wasn't something I was ready to deal with—I always figured that the weight would somehow disappear by the time I became an adult and was ready to start "my life." In the meantime, I accepted being the funny friend, the person guys talked to and laughed with— but never dated—and I hid behind long skirts and loose tops. Then in October 2002, when I was a senior in high school, my grandfather was diagnosed with cancer of the esophagus, and died three months later. His life was snuffed out so unexpectedly that it made me realize I couldn't wait around for "my life" to start. After his funeral, I promised myself that I was going to do whatever I could to start losing weight.

My diet wasn't all that revolutionary—I cut out all junk food and walked on the treadmill in my parents' basement every day—but it *did* work: By the time I went to a freshman orientation at Baruch College in May 2003, I'd lost 15 pounds. I was proud of what I'd started, but I didn't feel any better about myself. After all, I still had a long way to go. So when I sat next to a cute guy at orientation named Aren and said, "What's up?" I wasn't surprised that all he did was smile, say hi back—and then get up to talk to someone else.

TOTAL TRANSFORMATION

By April 2004, I'd lost 40 pounds. I finally thought I looked great, even sexy—and that gave me a huge surge of self-esteem. Guys were starting to pay attention to me; they made eye contact, smiled at me, and complimented me on what I was wearing. It felt awesome!

That month, one of my friends from school was having a party that I was really looking forward to. I put on a frilly little skirt that I *never* would have worn when I was heavier. At the party, I saw Aren, the cute guy from orientation—but this time, he looked at me for what felt like forever and then slowly smiled. I was freaking

66 That one moment made me feel gorgeous for a week. 99

out inside—I'd waited for years for someone to gaze at me that way. He walked over and said, "You look amazing tonight." I smiled and replied, "Thanks." But

26

before I could continue, he had to go help his friend with something. I barely got to talk to him again that night, but that one moment made me feel gorgeous for a week!

Over the next few months, Aren and I flirted a lot—but nothing romantic happened between us. Was he always going to see me as the fat girl from orientation? I wondered. Even though I really liked him, it looked like we'd never move beyond being friends. Then in December 2004, I used most of my savings to spend my winter break in Italy, visiting friends. While I was there, I sent an e-mail to another friend, telling her how much I missed Aren. She wrote me back: "You know he likes you, right?" I'd wanted to hear that for more than a year.

NEW CONFIDENCE

When I came back from Italy, I decided to talk to Aren about what was going on between us. "I thought you were cute from the moment I saw you," he said. I was shocked! I never thought he could be into me when I was heavy. Then he said, "But over the past year, you've turned into this confident person, and it made me like you more." That's when I knew I *had* changed: I was more outgoing and smiled more. I realized I'd been holding myself back. I'd *always* deserved the attention, no matter how heavy I was—I just had to believe it to get it.

Aren ended up transferring to another school, so we decided it was best to just stay friends. But I'll always wonder what would have happened if, on that first day we met, I had thought more of myself.

her love (don't cost a thing)

Sarah, 20, thought Ed came from "the wrong part of town." But then she realized that a guy from a completely different place could make her feel totally at home.

I grew up in Commack on Long Island, New York—where BMWs line people's driveways, girls can spot a fake Coach bag from a mile away, and all the guys wear A|X Armani Exchange. It was like I lived in a bubble, separate from the real world—but I was happy there. My parents always made sure I had everything I wanted, and so did the guys I dated.

BIG DIFFERENCE

In September 2003 I started college at Stony Brook University. On my first day of Business 110, a tall, cute guy (with cornrows!) came up to me. "What's good, ma? This seat taken?" he asked. "No," I said, surprised—I'd never met a guy who looked or talked like that. He sat down and continued, "Where you from?" After I told him, he said he was from Brentwood—and I went silent.

29

You see, Brentwood is just 10 minutes from my town, but it's a world away. I'd always heard that it's poor—filled with crime, gangs, and drugs. I had never met anyone from Brentwood—and I didn't really want to.

> **66 Did we *really* have things in common? What would my friends say? 99**

But he kept talking. "What happened to your arm?" he asked, pointing to a scrape. "I play softball . . ." I explained. "Really? I'm a pitcher on the baseball team," he said. I was shocked. I thought he'd sell *drugs*, not play *baseball*.

As we kept talking, I found out that his name was Ed, and that he was very funny. But honestly I still figured that he must be in a gang or something.

MUTUAL AGREEMENT

Ed barely came to class, but over the next three months I'd occasionally see him on campus. We'd smile and say hi—sort of like flirting. Then one December night, I ran into him outside my dorm. "Long time, no see," I said—and he surprised me with a high five and hug. "What's good with you for the night?" he asked. I told him I was going to watch a movie, and he said that he'd be into a movie. I was a little nervous that he just wanted to hook up, but he seemed so nice I decided to invite him in.

We went to my friend's room to watch *Scary Movie 3*. She fell asleep, but Ed and I stayed up, talking nonstop. Gradually he admitted that he'd had a crush on me since the day we met—he even remembered what I had been wearing! Finally, at about 3 A.M., we started getting tired, so Ed walked me back to my room—and offered to walk me to class the next day! He said it so sincerely—it was the sweetest thing I'd ever heard.

I began to get excited but also nervous. Did we *really* have things in common? What would my friends say?

At 9:30 the next morning, Ed showed up. It was pouring, but he walked me the whole way—even giving me piggybacks over puddles! Once we got to my class, he gave me his number, said, "Don't forget to call," and kissed me on the lips. I had never felt so taken care of.

PERFECT FIT

From then on, Ed and I hung out almost every night. I was happier than ever—but still hesitant. My parents' opinions mean a lot to me, and I wasn't sure they'd approve—I was afraid they'd think a Brentwood guy would just use me or cheat on me. So only two weeks after our first kiss, I brought Ed home. To my parents' credit, they didn't give us a hard time. I was so relieved.

Still, I wasn't ready to tell my best friend, Krista. She grew up near me and expects a guy to have a lot of money, so he can buy you things—and I was so afraid she'd try to convince me that I shouldn't be with Ed. But I hated having a secret, so a month after I began dating Ed, I introduced them at a party and told her we were dating. As I had feared, she said I could do better.

Krista's reaction upset me, but it didn't make me like Ed less—and we've now been together for a year. And what it's made me realize is that where a guy comes from and what others think of him just doesn't matter. What's important is how that person makes you feel.

31

i ran away to the middle east

Katherine, 17, fled the country to marry a guy she fell for on Myspace.com—and made international news. Now, she tells her side of the story.

i was into a rock band called Disturbed and decided to check out their MySpace page in mid-December 2005. As I looked through their friends' profiles, I came across a girl who had tattoos on her face and a unique style. I was intrigued and clicked on her page. At the top of *her* friend list, I saw this really cute guy named Abdullah. He had a warm smile and the most beautiful eyes—so I clicked on his picture and found out that he lived in the West Bank. I thought it would be cool to learn about his homeland and culture because I'd seen stories on the news about the fighting over there. Abdullah had posted in his profile that he loved hard-core rock bands, his mom's pizza, and chocolate. He also said he'd never had a girlfriend—which was *sweet!* I thought that might mean he had values and didn't date just any girl who came along. I typed, "You're really cute," and pressed "Send."

33

NEW LOVE

Two days later I got a reply. "Thanks. Your page looks nice," Abdullah wrote. We started chatting online for hours about our families, friends, and hobbies. I felt really comfortable with him, so we exchanged personal e-mail addresses. I'd had a boyfriend before, but Abdullah was different from any guy I'd ever liked. He asked all kinds of questions to get to know me—about my favorite songs, authors, and cities— and he really seemed to like me for who I was. He also was respectful and family-oriented, which I thought was amazing for a guy who was 20.

66 I felt I could tell him stuff I hadn't ever told anyone. 99

We had so much in common: We liked the same music, food, and books. We just *clicked*. I felt I could tell him stuff I hadn't ever told *anyone*, and he was never judgmental.

In early January, after sending e-mails to each other for a few weeks, Abdullah asked me for my phone number—and said he'd call that night. When my cell phone rang, my heart started pounding so loud I could hear it!

I was nervous—but *so* excited. "Hello," I said. He hesitated and then said softly, "Hi, this is Abdullah." I began to giggle—and he did too. We talked for *three* hours. He had an accent but his English was perfect. Before hanging up, I blurted out, "I love you." He replied, "Aw, I love you too." I didn't tell anyone about Abdullah except my 15-

year-old stepsister, Jordyn—and I made her promise
not to tell. I was just scared that everyone would
think I was crazy for getting involved with an
absolute stranger I'd met online. Abdullah and I
started talking several times a day—for an hour,
then 30 minutes, then another hour—*every* day.
Because we were talking so much, I started
sneaking around the house so no one would notice—
I'd go to the garage or the basement, or even sit in
the car in our driveway—but my mom still became
suspicious. One day she asked, "Who are you
talking to all the time?" I knew she wouldn't
understand, so I lied and told her it was just my
best friend, Brittany.

Over the next few weeks, Abdullah and I got to
know each other better and became best friends. But
I knew this was more than just a friendship—I
thought about him constantly and waited for his
calls. I was crazy in love and hoped he felt the same.
Then in late January, Abdullah asked, "Will you
marry me?" I said, "*Yes!*"

BOTCHED PLAN

Abdullah and I continued to talk almost every day. "I
can't wait until you're 18 so you can come to Israel to
visit me," he said in March. "That would be great," I
responded, thinking I'd have an entire year to save up
the money. Then a second later he said, "I don't want
to wait. I *really* want to see you. You can come here
now and we can get married." At first I hesitated. I
live in Gilford, Michigan—this tiny town surrounded
by cornfields—and I hadn't even traveled outside the
state that much. I couldn't *imagine* going halfway
across the globe.

But I realized I didn't want to wait either. "I can come when school lets out in June," I said excitedly. "You have to tell your parents about me first," he cautioned. "But if I tell them, they'll take my phone and computer away," I replied. He seemed frustrated that I refused, but he didn't press the issue.

After we hung up, I went on the Internet to look into traveling abroad and learned that I needed a passport. Since I was under 18, I had to have an adult fill out the form in order for me to get one. So I lied and told my mom that Brittany had invited me on a trip to Canada with her family. I felt horrible about lying, but all I thought about was finally getting to be with Abdullah.

66 I was screaming inside as my plan slowly fell apart. 99

After I got my passport in May, I went to the Greyhound station to buy a ticket to New York; Abdullah wired money to his cousin who lived in the Bronx so he could buy me a plane ticket to fly to Israel the first week of June. Abdullah planned to have his mom pick me up at the Tel Aviv airport when my plane landed so she could drive me to the West Bank.

Over the next month I gathered together all my stuff for the trip. I packed my passport, birth certificate, and enough clothes for two weeks. Abdullah's mom, who was helping us plan our wedding, had told me to bring a pink dress for the engagement party and a white one for the ceremony. The day before my trip, I was so anxious and excited that I could hardly sleep or eat.

On June 4, my mom drove me to the bus station,

where I'd told her Brittany's family was picking me up
for the trip to Canada. I had hoped she'd just drop me
off—but she insisted on waiting. "I'll be fine, Mom. You
can leave now," I said. "I want to talk with her parents
first to make sure you have everything you need," she
replied. I was screaming inside as my plan slowly fell
apart. Finally after 30 minutes of waiting, I told her
that we should just go. "Maybe they left without me,"
I said. Once we got in the car, I cried the whole
way home.

An hour later Abdullah called. As I told him what
had happened, I started crying again; he was crying
too. "Why don't you just tell your mom about us?" he
pleaded. But I refused. I was too afraid that if I told
her, I'd lose him.

ROAD TRIP

I got up the next morning even *more* determined to
see Abdullah. So when he called to ask how I was
doing, I just suddenly said, "I'm on my way!"—
I don't know what had come over me. I was still
packed, so I called a taxi and quickly got dressed.
My mom was at my grandmother's house, so I left
her a note saying I was staying the night with
Brittany. When I got to the station at 10 A.M., I asked
the clerk at the window what time the next bus to
New York was leaving—she said 11. After boarding
the bus, I sat in silence, staring out the window and
thinking, I can't believe I'm *actually* on a bus headed
to New York. It was surreal. I called my mom from the
bus midafternoon, just to tell her I was okay. "Where
are you?" she demanded. She had called Brittany to
ask if I was staying with her—and found out I'd lied.
By now I was really disgusted with myself for lying

and hurting my mom and dad by running away. I knew they'd be worried sick, and I kept asking myself, What am I *doing*? But I lied to her again, saying that I was at *another* friend's house—and told myself that I was doing this all for love.

The trip took 20 hours, and I had to change buses *five* times. I was so wired, I couldn't sleep. At 7 A.M. the next morning, I called my mom—and again she insisted that I tell her where I was. A police officer was at the house, and she put him on the phone. "Your parents are concerned about your safety, Katherine," he said. "You need to come home." I hung up on him.

> **66 Next thing I knew the plane was moving—it was too late to turn back. 99**

After I arrived in New York at 8 A.M., I met up with Abdullah's cousin and stayed the night with his family. It felt a little awkward, but Abdullah called the house every hour to make sure I was okay. The next evening they drove me to the airport.

GROWING PANIC

I had been ignoring the calls coming into my cell phone since I left home. But after I boarded the plane to Tel Aviv, I decided to listen to my messages—and that was when I found out that my stepsister, Jordyn, had confessed to my dad and stepmom that I knew a guy who lived in the West Bank. They had checked my computer and found my e-mails to Abdullah. "Please don't go to Israel," my stepmom, Krista, pleaded in her voice message. "There's a war going on over there!"

38

While I was listening to Krista's message, my phone started ringing. I answered it, and the man on the other end told me he was the sheriff of a town near Gilford. "You need to come home—*now*," he said sternly. "I'll be home as soon as I can," I lied. I told him my phone's battery was dying—and hung up. Now I was *really* scared. For a split second, I thought about turning back—then I remembered that Abdullah had paid $2,000 for my plane ticket. I didn't want him to waste the money. Next thing I knew the plane was moving—it was too late to turn back.

After a 12-hour flight, I arrived in Amman, Jordan, where I had to change planes to get to Tel Aviv. I immediately bought a phone card and called Abdullah to tell him I was okay. I boarded the next plane, then breathed a sigh of relief as it started rolling away from the gate—but then it suddenly stopped. I thought we were just delayed—until two airport security guards came onto the plane and one of them asked out loud, "Is there a Katherine Lester on board?" I held up my hand and the guard came over to my seat. He asked to see my passport. I handed it to him, and then he said I had to get off the plane.

SCARY MOMENT

I was *terrified*! My heart was beating faster than it ever had before, and my stomach was churning so badly that I thought I was going to throw up. The guards took me to an office, and I didn't know if I was under arrest—or if they were going to deport me. To my surprise, they asked me if I wanted something to drink and brought out tea. They started asking me about my hometown, my school, and the singer Shakira, which put me at ease. I couldn't believe it, but for almost an hour, we just talked and laughed, and they even taught me how to say a few words in Arabic. Then two American FBI agents walked in, and the mood completely changed. They said I'd been reported as a runaway. The guards handed them my passport, and the FBI agents told me I *had* to return to the United States.

BACK HOME

I sat in the airport for 13 hours, and since I was basically under arrest, there was no way for me to call Abdullah to let him know what had happened. By the time I was put on my flight back to New York, then to Flint, Michigan, I was so depressed—and tired—that I was almost relieved to be returning home. It had been five days since I left Gilford, and I just wanted to sleep in my own bed.

66 I had no idea until then that what I'd done had made international news. 99

When we landed at the airport in Flint, the FBI agents walked me off the plane directly onto the runway so I wouldn't have to go through the terminal and do a "perp walk" past all the television news cameras camping out there to get pictures of me. I had no idea until then that what I'd done had made international news.

My mom and dad were waiting in a car that was parked on the runway near the plane. I was so nervous—I had no clue how they would react. I honestly thought they might lock me in a room and not let me out until I turned 18! By the time I walked the short distance to the car, I'd started crying. My mom and dad hugged me, and they started crying too. "Why didn't you just tell me the truth?" my mom asked with tears in her eyes. "I thought you'd get upset," I said. "I'm sorry." My dad didn't say much—I could tell he was disappointed in me.

After we left the airport, we went to my dad's house and ordered pizza. I was so excited to see my little brother and sisters. We were all crying and laughing and hugging at the same time. My mom told me that while I was on my way back to Michigan, Abdullah— who I still hadn't spoken to since leaving to see him—had called her and apologized for all the trouble my trip had caused. I was glad he did that—and that she had finally talked with him. Though my parents were relieved that I was safe, they were also very angry. I kept apologizing and telling them how terrible I felt that I had hurt them so much, but most of all, I felt really sad that I had lost their trust.

The next day news reporters kept calling my mom's house and ringing the doorbell, trying to interview me. My mom didn't think it was a good idea for me to talk to anyone yet, so she sent me to stay with my dad, near Flint.

MORE TROUBLE

Two weeks after I got home, the local district attorney filed a runaway juvenile petition charge against me. I was *so* scared—I thought they might put me in a juvenile detention center.

41

On June 29, 2006, I had to appear in family court in Caro, Michigan. I really thought I was going to get in a lot of trouble, but my dad came with me and kept reassuring me the whole time that it would all be okay. Even though I *had* broken the law, the district attorney dropped the charges after I agreed to surrender my passport until I turn 18, finish high school, and complete a counseling program. I also had to promise not to leave the state without having my parents' written permission.

❝ I understand what I did was wrong, so now I'm working really hard to win back their trust . ❞

While my parents were very supportive through the legal issues, I can see how much our relationship has changed because of what I did—both in good ways *and* bad. No matter how many times I say I'm sorry, I still can't get back their trust. Now they're always calling me during the day to make sure I really am where I say I'm going to be. Plus, they're constantly looking over my shoulder whenever I'm on the Internet. I understand what I did was wrong, so now I'm working really hard to win back their trust. Now I always tell them the truth because I realize that if I'm lying about something, it means I probably shouldn't be doing it.

Abdullah and I still talk on the phone every day for at least one hour. Although a lot of people—

including my parents—don't believe us, we really do love each other and we *are* going to get married someday. Love is full of tests, and we're going to pass ours. I know it.

the not-quite boyfriend

Rachel, 19, was afraid to end her relationship—
even when things got ugly.

ace and I started dating in January 2002, my sophomore year of college. He was different from the guys I usually liked. While my last boyfriend never went to college and didn't really have plans for his future, Ace was polite, smart, and motivated. One night a few weeks after our first date, he was walking me home after dinner when he turned and said, "You *know* I like you, right?" Flattered, I replied, "Sure, I like you too." After a few moments, he nervously stammered, "Will you be my girlfriend?" I said, "Of course!" I was excited that we were officially a couple and that my friends and family were finally going to approve of my boyfriend. *This* is the kind of person I should be with, I thought.

BELIEVING A LIE

For the first month, Ace and I were really happy together. He would take me out to dinner a couple of times a week and call each evening to say good night— his attention made me feel beautiful and gave me a boost of confidence. But what I loved most about being with Ace was that I never had to worry about having no plans or feeling lonely on the weekends: I had a boyfriend, so there would always be someone there for me.

Then in late March, Ace got really stressed about his grades and started canceling a lot of our dates so he could study. I began to notice that the only time he *did* call was when he wanted to have sex—but I thought it would only be a temporary thing. Then one morning at 3 A.M., when we were lying next to each other in his bed, Ace said, "You need to go. I have to get up early."

I was horrified—he totally made me feel like I was just a booty call. I told him I didn't want to be treated like crap.

> 66 **Even though he was using me, the truth was that I was using him too.** 99

"What do you want from me?" he yelled back. So I threw on my clothes and stormed out.

As I walked back to my dorm, I kept thinking about what a jerk he was and that I *had* to dump him. But then reality hit: I liked being in a relationship, and the thought of not having Ace—not having *anyone*—completely terrified me. Even though he was using me, the truth was that I was using him too. I just wasn't ready yet to give up being someone's girlfriend. So I stayed with Ace and hoped he would eventually start behaving better.

FACING THE TRUTH

We were together for the next two years, even though he continued to want me mostly for the physical stuff. I wasn't that happy in the relationship, but when Ace would call and ask me to stop by, it made me feel so good that I'd forget all the bad things he'd done to me—and rush right over to see him.

Then, at the end of our senior year in May 2004, my friends and I were out at a club when Ace showed up with a girl I didn't know. He didn't see me, but I watched him pull her onto the dance floor and start kissing her. When he finally glanced across the room and noticed me, he looked shocked for a second but then just turned away and kept dancing. My heart dropped. I was furious, and at that moment, it clicked how little Ace actually cared about me. And I had to ask myself if being on my own could be any worse than being totally humiliated like this.

BREAKING IT OFF

The next afternoon, Ace called to apologize. But I cut him off midsentence and said, "We shouldn't see each other ever again." Then I hung up. He tried to reach me a few times over the next month, but I refused to answer.

It was hard to admit that I wasted more than two years of my life being treated badly by someone who was never a true boyfriend. But now that I'm single, I have a lot of fun and get to spend more time with the people who do respect and love me—and I don't miss Ace at all!

the
accidental
virgin

Jessica, 21, didn't *plan* on waiting
this long to "lose it"—but true love hasn't
come her way yet.

i 'll just get to the point. I'm 21 and still a virgin. I
have had many loves in my life: my family, three
best friends, three cats, two hamsters, one dog,
and a pair of pink patent leather stilettos. But with the
exception of my dad and my hamster Cottonball, that
list does not include any guys. To put it simply, I've
been surrounded by love—but I've never been *in* love.

I didn't think much of it until last year; but now that
I'm a junior in college, it has started to really bother
me that I have never had sex. I didn't make a conscious
decision to abstain. I fully plan on having sex with
more than one person in my lifetime. In my opinion,
premarital sex is fine (although I know not everyone
feels that way). When I discussed this with my best
friend, I came to the conclusion that while being with
more than one guy is perfectly acceptable, four is a
good limit. Five is dangerous: That's an entire hand's
worth, and from there, the double digits (which I don't

think I can handle) are a mere few fingers away. So anyway, I have nothing against sex, but here's the catch: I do want to be in love the first time I have it. And falling in love is something that I have not quite gotten to on my lifetime to-do list.

THE COLLEGE PLAN

My early romances suggested that I'd be an early bloomer. My first crush came in third grade. Our one and only date was a movie (*The Sandlot*—my mom not only chaperoned, she sat between us). Then came my first kiss (sixth grade), first make-out session (tenth grade), and my first real boyfriend (twelfth grade—but he just wasn't "the one"). The whole time I figured that when I got to college, I would fall in love and have a wonderful first-sex experience freshman year. When that didn't happen, I began to worry. The problem was not that I didn't have opportunities— I had plenty—it was that I didn't fall in love. I wasn't looking for the love of my life, but I did want to share the moment with someone I could trust, who gave me butterflies, who wouldn't leave and never talk to me again—someone I could look back on and not regret.

Maybe I've put too much emphasis on having sex for the first time. Perhaps the elusive moment isn't that big a deal. Maybe it's like senior prom—something you hold to an impossibly high standard but that is in reality just another experience that will come and go. Still, I can't help but think that losing my virginity is a milestone that will irrevocably change my life.

THE WAITING GAME

As college continued, my fellow virgins dropped off one by one, and most of my friends who abstained planned

50

to wait for marriage. I began to wonder, Is love too high a standard for sex? Should I settle for *like*?

The question stuck with me. One night, when I was back home in Kansas City, Kansas, a close guy friend and I started making out, and I couldn't stop thinking about it. We have never dated each other, and neither of us wants to, but I trust and respect him—and we hook up on occasion. So this time, while we were kissing, I started to think: Maybe I should just get it over with and do it now. After all, we've gone most of the way in the past without much awkwardness. And I know that I wouldn't be just some random girl for him—we've been friends for years. Maybe sex is just one step further. But then again, it might be a giant leap. Then came a more disturbing thought: If I'm able to think this analytically about whether I want to sleep with this guy while we're actually making out, maybe he *really* isn't the right person. And furthermore, do I want my first time to be on a futon in my parents' basement while the dog is scratching at the door? Then I wondered if my mom was home and if the movie we had started watching would rewind itself after the credits. Actually, I wondered how the movie ended. . . . Maybe there is a point where *like* meets *love*, but we were definitely not there.

THE ROAD AHEAD

In the end, I did not settle for like. If I can't settle for the almost-right winter coat, I certainly can't settle for the almost-right guy. I realize that my first time will probably not be with my forever true love, but I still want that possibility. I want the butterflies and anticipation and completely giddy feeling I've heard so much about. So for now, I will remain an accidental— but highly optimistic—virgin.

surviving a breakup

When Heather, 20, got dumped, she fell apart. But then she figured out how to get over her ex—*and* feel good again.

When Jamie asked me out in the summer of 2001, I couldn't believe such a hot guy was talking to *me*. Of course I said yes, and after just one date, I was falling in love. Although I was 16 and a junior in high school, and he was starting his second year at a college more than 2,000 miles away, we were sure we could make things work long-distance. Over the next year, we'd talk on the phone for hours each day and spend every minute together when he came home on break. In the summer of 2002, Jamie told me some great news—in the fall, he was transferring to a school closer to me so we could see each other more!

BITTER ENDING

Everything was amazing between us—until he started hanging out with his ex. Jamie assured me they were just friends, but I'd get so jealous over her that we'd fight a lot throughout the year. Then one night in August 2003, I was with one of my guy friends. I knew he liked me, but I never wanted to date him. He and I were sitting on the sofa when he leaned in to kiss me. I froze but then kissed him back. After a few seconds, I pulled away. "That was wrong," I said. My friend tried to calm me down, but I was freaked out. Sure, I was having trouble with Jamie, but I still *loved* him—I didn't want this kiss to ruin it!

A few weeks later, I went to visit Jamie at school— I was happy to see him, even though it felt like all we did was fight. I didn't think he'd find out about the kiss, but Jamie knew my friend and I were hanging out—and was totally jealous! "You're with him all the time!" Jamie yelled. "Nothing's going on!" I insisted. But Jamie refused to believe me, and we barely spoke that weekend. I left on Sunday scared that our relationship was collapsing. When I got home, Jamie called. "Are you *sure* you never hooked up with him?" he asked. "I swear," I lied. "I logged on to your IM pretending I was you," Jamie said, "and asked him if he remembered the time we hooked up. He said *yes*." My heart dropped—and I knew I had to tell the truth. "It was just a *kiss*," I insisted. "I can't believe you'd do this," Jamie said. "It's over." Then he hung up.

FALLING APART

I couldn't believe it. I called Jamie six times in a row but only got his voice mail—so I left messages begging him to take me back. I thought I was dying, like my heart had been ripped out. I curled up in bed and cried.

I kept calling, but Jamie didn't call back until three days later. "I had sex with another girl," he said. "Sorry, but you need to know it's over." I was crushed—I couldn't deal with him being with someone else after he'd been mine for two years. I stayed in bed for the next two weeks and wouldn't eat. My weight dropped from 100 pounds to 78. My parents were terrified—they checked me into the hospital for three weeks, and the doctors prescribed antidepressants.

I called Jamie from my hospital bed—he just said, "Sorry you're not feeling well." His coldness made me angry. "Forget it," I snapped, and slammed down the phone. For the next few days, I went back and forth between missing and hating him.

SLOW RECOVERY

When I left the hospital, my best friend, Savannah, called to check up on me. "Do not contact him for three months," she said. "No way!" I cried, still not ready to let go. "Call him and our friendship's over," she said. So I agreed—but never thought I could do it. She came over the next day, erased his numbers from my phone, and blocked his e-mail address from my account.

As the weeks went by, the pain got better. When I wanted to call Jamie, I'd call Savannah instead. It was months before I could go a whole day without thinking of him. Almost two years later, I feel better and am finally having fun again. I *do* get lonely, but I now know that all the jealousy between Jamie and me wasn't healthy—we never learned to really trust each other. I won't make the same mistake with a guy again.

yo-yo dating

Every time Brianna, 17, decides she has finally had it with her boyfriend, Jake, he sucks her back in. Sound familiar?

t his past year has been a roller coaster. In February 2003 I started going out with Jake. He'd told a friend that he thought I was hot, and I said I thought he was hot too, and I'd consider going on a date with him. Pretty soon we were talking on the phone three or four times a week, and I'd go over to his house like once a week to watch movies in his basement. We got along really well. He'd tell me that he liked me so much, and his friends said it too. One of my guy friends who plays soccer with Jake told me, "He never stays with his girlfriends, but I can tell he really likes you. He talks about you differently."

Jake was my first *boyfriend* boyfriend, so that probably made *me* like *him* a lot more too. I kind of thought that we were going to last forever. But I guess I should have seen that it was more of *me* in the relationship than him. This was a typical Jake move: He would call and ask, "You wanna do something tonight?" So I wouldn't make any plans, and I'd wait to hear from him for hours. Then I'd finally call his house, and his mom would be like, "Oh, he's already gone."

THE FIRST BREAKUP

In May we went to Jake's senior prom. A few weeks later, this girl in his class told me that he had asked her to come over and go in his hot tub with him. (She didn't go.) So I confronted him at school, and he denied the whole thing. Then he said he had to go to class and we'd talk about it later. I didn't believe him at all. I was so mad. That night on the phone he asked, "Do you think we should be together, since I'm going away to college and everything?" I told him no, I didn't want to deal with this anymore, because I didn't know what else to say. So we broke up.

> **66 I didn't want to deal with this anymore—so we broke up. 99**

The next couple of weeks I wasn't myself at all. I had trouble eating and sleeping. I couldn't get over him. All summer I hung out with his best friend's girlfriend, Ashley, so I could see Jake more—we'd be at the same parties and he'd flirt with me. Then he'd call me and ask if I wanted to come over to his house, and I'd always go.

A RANDOM RETURN

We didn't talk for about a month after the school year started. Then he started randomly calling me again—late at night, on my cell. (I have the phone next to my bed so I always hear it.) He always seemed to call when he was drunk or at parties. One time he said he wanted me to go to his college so we could get back together and someday get married! And even though I wanted to go to Indiana University, I would find myself thinking maybe I *could* go to his school instead.

In mid-October he asked if I ever thought about getting back together. I wanted to say, "Are you serious? I think about it every day!" But instead I simply said yes. He asked if I thought we should try it again. I asked *him* if it would be like last time, like when I'd never hear from him. He said no—but then didn't call once the whole next week.

That's when I broke up with Jake. I told him that he didn't understand how to treat girls, that he was too scared to be with someone who really cared about him and who he cared about too. He got really quiet. He knew it was true, and I think it actually surprised him that I said it.

BACK FOR MORE

This cycle will never end—two weeks later we started talking again. But now he's actually been calling me when he says he will. One night he started to sort of open up and tell me how he felt. He said I was the only girl he ever felt this strongly about, and he didn't know why he didn't keep me. He thought it might be because he didn't want to be "tied down"— and that kind of scared him.

But here's the thing: I like him so much! I *want* to believe that Jake wants us to be together. But I don't know if I can trust him anymore and that scares me . . . because I want to trust him *so* bad.

a love triangle

After Robert decided to fight in Iraq, his girlfriend Ashley, 19, fell in love with his brother. Is following her heart worth destroying a family?

robert was my very first love. He and I started dating in 2000, when I was 14 and he was 15. I was so happy for the first five months, but then he became too clingy, always calling to check up on me and acting jealous of my guy friends. I tried hard to make it work, but after nine months, I decided to break up with him. Even though I didn't want him as a boyfriend, I still wanted him in my life. We ended up staying really close, but I didn't think I still loved him romantically— until he told me in the summer of 2003 that he was joining the Marines.

SAD GOODBYE

It was July, and Robert had just graduated from high school. We were driving back to his house after seeing a movie, and I was talking about how excited I was to start my senior year. "I signed up for the Marines," Robert suddenly said. "I'm leaving in a month." I was so shocked that I sat in silence for a minute. "I guess it'll be good for you," I finally said, knowing he didn't want to go to college. Then I began thinking that he might be sent to Iraq and killed—and I felt nauseous. The idea of Robert not being there for me made me realize how much I cared for him. "Will you miss me?" he asked. "You know I will," I replied, and started to cry.

> 66 **The more I got to know Richard, the more I became attracted to him. But my feelings horrified me.** 99

For the next few weeks, we were a couple again and spent every day together. But then, in August, Robert had to leave for his 13-week boot camp in Parris Island, South Carolina. I went to his house the day before he took off, and we sat on his sofa for hours, holding each other. "It's so unfair that you have to leave now that we've gotten close again," I said. With Robert gone, I didn't know who I was going to lean on.

NEW LOVE

That fall, I hung out a lot with my friend Jonathan, who was close with Robert's brother, Richard. Richard, a 15-year-old sophomore, was three years younger than me. The three of us would watch movies or sit around and talk. The more I got to know Richard, the more I became attracted to him—I loved his sarcastic sense of humor and how he always just said whatever was on his mind. But my feelings horrified me. I would think to myself, How could you fall for your boyfriend's *brother*? It was such a betrayal. But Robert no longer felt like a boyfriend—after boot camp, he was stationed 3,000 miles away at Camp Pendleton in California and wasn't around to give me attention.

> **66 I wasn't thinking about Robert, or how much this would hurt him. 99**

One day in May 2004, after Robert had been gone for six months, Richard and I were at his house. We were lying on his mom's bed, talking about our plans for the night, when he sat up and leaned over me. My heart started pounding. He moved his head closer to mine and when our lips touched, I wasn't thinking about Robert or how much this would hurt him, I was just excited because this kiss meant that Richard liked me back.

BIG LIE

Richard and I were inseparable for the next three months. And even though I was in love with him, the guilt about Robert was making me sick. Robert and I were still talking on the phone once a week, though I was starting to push him away. But I didn't tell him about Richard yet—I just wasn't ready to deal with his pain and anger. One afternoon in August 2004, I finally told Robert straight out that we should go back to being friends. He begged me to reconsider and said, "They're sending me to Iraq. I need you to be there for me." My heart dropped because I knew how much danger he'd be in. I really didn't want him to go. "I'll be here for you," I said. I couldn't tell

> **"Robert will be back home soon, and I know that I have to tell him everything when he returns."**

him about Richard *then*. I didn't want him to be upset about the stuff happening back home when he had to go to war.

While Robert was overseas, their mom started asking why Richard and I were spending so much time together, so we finally told her about our relationship. She got really angry at first and said, "I can't believe you both would hurt Robert like this." But when she saw how happy we were, she promised not to break the news to her son.

Richard and I have been together for almost a year—and I feel closer to him than I ever did to Robert. But Robert will be back home soon, and I know that I have to tell him everything when he returns. I just hope he understands that I never meant to hurt him. But I can't help who I like— and I deserve to be happy too.

the
conquest

**When Samantha, 22, met Jeremy, she decided she'd
do anything to get him—and learned that sometimes,
winning the prize isn't all it's cracked up to be . . .**

i 've always been competitive, so when I got
to Barnard College in 2003, I thought
joining the fencing team would be a good
way to meet people. I was excited to talk to my
teammates, but at the preseason dinner, I found
myself focusing on just one person: Jeremy, the
captain. He held himself with such confidence. He
was the hottest guy on the team, maybe in the
whole school. I was both drawn to him and a little
intimidated—he was an upperclassman *and* the
first college guy I'd ever talked to. When he sat
down next to me and asked, "How do you like
college?" all I could manage to say was a lame "Um,
it's good so far."

A few weeks later I overheard a girl on the
team tell another girl, "I've like Jeremy *forever*, but
nothing is ever gonna happen." My ears perked up as
I heard her friend reply, "He could be with any girl.
But that's the problem—he knows it." So *everyone*
thought Jeremy was unattainable. Then I said to
myself, I've never turned down a challenge before. . . .
I'll make him mine.

PLAYING TO WIN

From that day on, I spent as much time as I could with Jeremy. I asked him to help me improve my fencing strategy at practice and sat by him on all of our team's bus trips. But as hard as I tried, I couldn't get him to loosen up at all. Any *other* guy would have gotten the hint, but Jeremy was totally oblivious. So when I saw him at a party that April, I knew I had to be more direct. "Since the season's over, we should hang out sometime," I said casually. He paused for a second and then replied, "Sure — but *you'll* have to call *me*. With a laugh I said, "You'll have to give me your number then." (Hey, if he wanted me to take charge, I was up for it!)

66 I kept thinking, I *can't* let the night end without something happening. 99

I wasted no time. When I left the party a few hours later, I called to see if he wanted to grab a bite. Next thing I knew we were at a diner near campus ordering food. But once I got him there, I was nervous: I didn't know if he was really interested. I tried to chat about fencing, but Jeremy didn't say much. After we ate, when he was walking me home, I kept thinking, I *can't* let the night end without something happening — this is my *one* shot at getting him. So I just went for it and kissed him. At first he froze and didn't kiss back — but when he did, it was the best kiss of my life. I truly felt like I'd won a prize.

FALSE START

Jeremy and I saw each other three times in the next three weeks. But I always had to initiate it—he *never* called me. We'd meet at parties, then go home together and hook up. Nothing else had worked, so I thought being physically close might make us emotionally close too. Each time I saw him I'd try asking him questions about himself, but he'd give one-word responses—it was *so* frustrating. I *knew* there was more to him: I saw how great he was to his friends and how supportive he was to the team. I thought, I've come *this* far—I know I can make it work.

One night my sophomore year, Jeremy and I were lying in bed after having sex. I couldn't take the silence, so I asked, "What's going on with us?" He pulled away and said, "Well, I don't want to be your *boyfriend*—but we're having fun, right?" I said, "Sure," but it was a lie. I wanted more, and now I knew my dream was hopeless.

TRUE VICTORY

Soon after, I told Jeremy we shouldn't see each other anymore, knowing he'd just say, "You're right—we shouldn't." And he did. But two months later he called to ask me to dinner. I figured he wanted to apologize for using me, so I said yes. When I showed up, he didn't say sorry—but he *did* talk about his family and his goals. I didn't know why he'd changed, but it was nice to be friends. Then one day, after we'd hung out for a few weeks, Jeremy kissed me. I was surprised—but I kissed him back. I had been so determined to be with him at first that I'd rushed in and settled for less than I deserved. But this time *he* was winning *me* over with something real—trust and respect. It took two tries, but now we're a solid team.

fighting like animals

Ashley loved how passionate Dillon was about her. But when that passion turned into rage, she knew she needed to let go.

In August 2004, at the start of my freshman year at Emory University, I was at a local club with my friends when this cute guy came up to me. "Hey, I'm Dillon," he said confidently. I smiled and replied, "Ashley." We began talking, and I found out that he was a freshman too. We chatted for a little while about where we were from and what music we liked—and then Dillon pulled my face toward his and began kissing me. I was startled by his aggressive move, but I didn't think about stopping him—the kiss was great! The boyfriend I had dated all through high school was super-shy, so I liked having a guy be this bold—he made it clear that he was into me! "That was nice," I said when it was over. Then Dillon took my number and promised to call. I couldn't wait!

INTENSE PASSION

Dillon called the next day, and we began hanging out about three times a week. He'd also text me each morning, saying things like, "I'm thinking of you." He was so take-charge—he'd assume, without asking, that we'd be spending the weekends together. I loved that he knew what he wanted: me.

Three months later I was in Dillon's dorm room showing him the Hanukkah gift I'd gotten from my dad—a $600 digital camera. "Cool," he said, looking at the photos I'd taken of friends in my dorm. Suddenly his face tensed up. "What are you doing with *this* guy?" he snarled, shoving the camera back at me. I looked and saw he was talking about my friend Max. "What do you mean?" I asked nervously. "He's a friend." Dillon had never raised his voice at me before—his face was so filled with rage, I felt like

> 66 **Dillon had never raised his voice at me before—his face was so filled with rage, I felt like he'd turned into a different person right in front of me.** 99

he'd turned into a different person right in front of me. Then he grabbed my upper arms and started shaking me, shouting, "You're a whore! This is over!" I just yelled, "Leave me alone! Don't touch me!" Dillon let go of my arms—but then he ripped the camera from my hands and flung it against

72

the wall, shattering it. "I can't believe you did that!" I screamed. Terrified by his rage, I began crying and ran back to my room. Immediately I called my best friend to tell her what had happened, and she told me I needed to end things. But as bad as it was, I felt like this fight had to be a fluke. Dillon was usually so caring—and I loved him.

ALWAYS ARGUING

The next morning I woke up to Dillon knocking on my door. "I want to apologize," he called out, sounding like the attentive guy I'd fallen in love with. I decided to let him in so he could explain what had happened the previous night. "I'm so sorry," he said. "I just love you so much." It touched me that he cared about me like that. I mean, even *after* I told him Max was just a friend, Dillon was *still* jealous. My first boyfriend loved me, but never showed me *this* much passion. So when Dillon asked if we could forget the fight, I agreed—and said I'd hang out with my guy friends less.

> **66** It touched me that he cared about me like that... My first boyfriend loved me, but never showed me *this* much passion. **99**

73

But near the end of freshman year, in May 2005, Dillon heard from one of his friends that I'd

> **I knew he cared about me...I hated all this friction, but I figured jealousy was part of having an intense love.**

had lunch alone with one of my guy friends. Dillon called that night and asked if it was true. When I said yes, he got angry and started yelling, which he'd been doing more and more. "You'd better never do that again!" he ordered. "I don't want you seeing other guys by yourself!" I was taken aback that he was being so demanding, but I knew it was just because he cared about me—so I promised I wouldn't. I hated all this friction, but I figured jealousy was part of having an intense love.

FINAL BLOWUP

Three weeks into sophomore year, Dillon called one night and invited me to his room. When I got there, I could tell he'd been drinking. "You should just go to sleep," I said. "Are you hooking up with other guys?" he asked out of nowhere. Stunned, I told him no. But he nodded and said, "You're such a whore!" Something in me snapped then, and I yelled, "I'm leaving—that's it!" He just stood there in total disbelief and let me walk out.

Six months later, Dillon and I are still broken up. We talk about getting back together, but he says he likes the freedom of not being in a relationship. I guess I'm not sure what I want—but I *do* know that I still care about him and always want him in my life.

saving himself

Sarah, 21, told Travis she wanted to lose her virginity to him—but he didn't feel the same way. Can their relationship survive his decision?

travis and I started casually dating in the fall of 2004, when we were both 20-year-old college juniors. We'd been friends for a few years, and I had a crush on him for most of that time—but I was too scared to make a move. Then one afternoon we were at my parents' house watching a movie, and he leaned over to me and confessed, "I'm starting to have feelings for you. I think we should try dating." Of course, I happily agreed.

By the spring of 2005, Travis and I were totally in love and hanging out every day. We'd pretty much done everything sexually except have intercourse, and I was beginning to think Travis was the guy I wanted to give my virginity to. I had waited to have sex because I wanted it to be with a guy I really loved and trusted, and I assumed Travis, who was a virgin too, was doing the same. Since we cared so much about each other, it made perfect sense for us to be each other's first.

BIG SURPRISE

One night in March, about five months after we began dating, we had been fooling around in Travis's room and were lying next to each other in his bed. When Travis pulled me into his arms and said, "I love you," in my ear, I knew it was the right time to tell him I was ready for us to have sex. So I turned toward him, lay down on top of him—and with my face inches from his, I whispered, "I want you to be my first."

I was sure he felt the same way, but after a few long seconds of silence, he softly replied, "Sarah, I *do* love you. But I take my religion seriously, and I want to wait until I'm married." My jaw dropped, and I rolled off of him. My boyfriend doesn't want to have *sex* with me? What's *wrong* with me, was all I could think. Guys don't turn down sex—*girls* say no.

> **It felt like there was a hole in my life.**

After a minute of silence, I sat up and asked, "You're *really* waiting until marriage?" He was quiet until I turned and faced him, and then he said, "I want to try."

I didn't know what to do, so I just lay back down, turned my back to him, and pretended to fall asleep. But my mind was racing—I was completely crushed to find out that Travis didn't think I was the one for him. Even though he always said he loved me, it suddenly felt like he didn't love me *enough*. I got scared that maybe our relationship wasn't as great as I thought—and that maybe I cared a lot more for him than he did for me.

SERIOUS DOUBTS

The next morning, Travis and I woke up and said nothing about the night before. He asked if I wanted to get breakfast, but I mumbled, "No," got dressed, and left. I just wanted to get back to my house on campus so I could talk to my roommates about what had happened. I felt so rejected and wondered if this meant Travis and I should break up. I really needed their advice.

But once I described the situation, my friends thought *I* was being completely unfair. "You can't tell him how he should be, just to make you happy," one said. "And haven't *you* said no to a lot of guys in the past?" They all agreed that if I loved Travis as much as I said I did, then I had to respect his decision.

Travis called me five times over the next four days, but I never picked up. I knew my friends were right, yet I still felt so hurt and disappointed that I wasn't ready to talk. Then, as the days went by, I missed him — Travis was my best friend, and I always shared every detail of my daily life with him. Without him, it suddenly felt like there was a hole in my life.

PURE LOVE

A week after I rushed out of his room, I felt so miserable without Travis that I had to call him. "Sorry I haven't been in touch," I said when he answered. "You just . . . *surprised* me." He sounded relieved and said, "I'm glad you called. It's not that I don't love you, but I have to follow my faith." When he said it that time, it finally clicked: This wasn't about me. Travis wouldn't have sex because he needed to stay true to his beliefs — and it was that devotion that I'd always loved about him.

I knew I wanted to be with him, even though I still felt a little hurt. "Let's figure out how to make this work," I said. Travis and I have now been together for nine months. Not having sex *is* hard, because I feel like I'm missing something great that everyone else is doing. But having Travis in my life is more important. And who knows — I still may end up being the one for him!

strung along

Lauren, 21, just *knew* she was the perfect girl for Mike—if only he'd open his eyes and see it too. But she learned the tough way that all the waiting and hoping in the world won't make a guy want to be your boyfriend.

i liked Mike right from our first conversation. We had gone to high school together in Belmont, California, but we didn't really meet until the summer of 2003 at a friend's party. He was funny and cute, and we began chatting regularly online and occasionally seeing each other at parties. At first we just talked about school and our part-time jobs. But after a month, he started getting flirtatious, telling me that I always looked so good or that he was hoping to see me out. The attention made me feel great.

On New Year's Eve of that year, Mike and I were at my friend Rachel's house. At midnight he grabbed me and said, "You're going to be my New Year's kiss," and we started making out. I knew right then that I wanted to be with him.

THE HEARTBREAK

That week, Mike and I were IMing back and forth, but neither of us brought up the kiss. I kept waiting for

81

him to ask me out, and I was trying to be patient. We had great chats, so I felt optimistic. Then one day he suddenly typed, "I have to sign off. I'm meeting my girlfriend." My heart plunged as I stared at the screen. But he was always flirting with *me*! How could he be dating someone *else*? I didn't want to appear psycho, so I casually responded, "Oh, when did you start seeing her?" He had already signed off, though. I felt numb—and I decided I shouldn't talk with him anymore. But the next day he IM'd me (*without* answering my question), and I got sucked back in, remembering how funny he was and how easy it was to talk to him. I hoped he'd break up with her and realize I was the right girl for him.

SLOW SEDUCTION

Mike and I flirted on and off for more than a year. Then one night in late August 2005, I met up with some friends at T.G.I. Friday's. Mike was there, looking pretty down. "What's wrong?" I asked him. "My girlfriend and I broke up," he said. "Oh, my God, I'm so sorry," I said, trying to sound sincere, although inside I was ecstatic. He didn't want to talk about it, but we made plans to hang out the next day. We had a great time, and I felt all this sexual tension between us.

> **❝ I know I should cut him out of my life, but I can't yet. ❞**

Later that night we were IMing when he typed, "Want to come over?" Uh, *yes*! "Okay," I replied. He's finally ready to be with me, I thought. I got in my car and practically broke speed records to get to his house.

"What's up?" I said when I got there. We made small talk but I couldn't take it anymore and I kissed him. One thing led to another, and we ended up having sex. It was exactly as I had pictured it. "I care about you so much," I told him as we were lying in bed afterward. I felt so in love. "Lauren, you're a good friend, but I just broke up with my girlfriend," he replied. My heart began to pound. "Well, do you see us going anywhere?" I asked hopefully, fearful of what his answer would be. "I don't know," he said simply. I was crushed. I got up, put on my clothes, and left without saying another word.

We didn't talk over the next week, and I began to realize I had made a huge mistake by sleeping with him. Then it got worse: I was out with some mutual friends, and I asked where Mike was. "Oh, he's back together with his girlfriend," one of the guys said. I almost threw up. He had used me as his "rebound" girl, but I was also furious at *myself* for being such an easy target.

PAINFUL MEMORY

Today Mike is still with his girlfriend. I stopped talking to him for a while, but we've recently started hanging out again. He continues to flirt with me and makes jokes about how we should sleep together again. He calls it "round two," which makes me feel gross. But I still care about him and feel so connected to him—he's addictive. I know I should cut him out of my life, but I can't yet. Maybe someday I'll be able to—and find the great boyfriend I deserve.

in love
with a girl

Natasha, 18, was always boy crazy—
until the day she met Jodi.

all through junior high, I *always* had a boyfriend. Anytime a relationship ended, I found a new guy within a week. But during freshman year of high school, in September 2002, that stopped. I still had fun hanging out with guys, but I didn't really feel attracted to them. Instead I sometimes caught myself checking out a cute *girl* I passed in the hallway. I figured it was just some sort of weird phase—and that if I ignored it, it would go away.

Seven months later, in April 2003, I was at church with my family when, during the sermon, I locked gazes with a girl who had amazing blue eyes. Something inside me just said, I *have* to meet her. So after the service, I walked over and introduced myself. She smiled and said, "My name's Jodi." We didn't get a chance to really talk, because she had to go—but I found myself thinking about her for days afterward.

SUDDEN REALIZATION

The thought had crossed my mind that I might be gay, but I couldn't deal with it. I mean, life is tough enough without having to question your sexuality, which just opens a whole can of worms I wasn't ready to face. But then that September, the beginning of sophomore year, an incredible thing happened: I transferred to Jodi's school. I hadn't seen her since that day at church, but she remembered me, which made me *so* happy. We made plans to go to a movie, and I began looking forward to it, almost like it was a *date*.

We got to the theater late, so we had to creep around in the dark to find seats. As we sat down our hands brushed, and suddenly this feeling came over me—I wanted to hold her hand so badly! I was scared by my attraction, so I crossed my arms in front of me and reminded myself that she was just a friend. After the movie, we took a short walk. She looked beautiful in the moonlight, and I felt another powerful urge to be close to her, but my fear took over again. I didn't say anything—and went home feeling miserable.

> **66 She looked beautiful in the moonlight, and I felt another powerful urge to be close to her, but my fear took over again. 99**

I knew it was time to admit I was gay. I worried what my friends would say, but I couldn't hold it in anymore. So I went to my friend Sarah. "Can we talk?" I asked her one day. "Sure, what's wrong?" she replied, looking concerned. "Nothing... But I have a secret. I think I'm a lesbian," I blurted out. "That's cool," she said, and shrugged. She was *shrugging*? I couldn't believe Sarah was so chill about it. Her reaction gave me confidence— maybe people would accept me even if I *was* different.

66 I had been so preoccupied dealing with my own stuff that I'd never considered that she might be gay, too. 99

So the next day, I was with a group of my friends, and I just came out to all of them. They were totally supportive. I felt like a huge weight had been lifted off me. But the big surprise was Jodi. After I told her, she replied, "I like girls, too." I couldn't believe it! I had been so preoccupied dealing with my *own* stuff that I'd never considered that *she* might be gay, too. We smiled and hugged—but I didn't reveal my crush on her. When I thought she was straight, I didn't have to worry about her rejecting me. But once I knew that she *wasn't*, I wondered, What if she doesn't feel about me the way I feel about her? It was safer not to know the answer.

NEW ROMANCE

For the next month, Jodi and I spent a lot of time together. I was falling in love with her—and trying to get up the courage to admit it. Then one day in October, we were at a park when Jodi took my hand. "There's something I need to tell you," she began nervously. "I love you." I was terrified she was just playing around, so like a dope I tried to play it cool. I said, "I'm sorry, I don't love you." Then I turned and ran home, crying.

> **❝ I'm so much happier now that I'm being honest about who I am. ❞**

I instantly regretted it. Jodi would never kid around about something so deep! I knew I *had* to tell her the truth. So that night I wrote her a poem, pouring out my feelings and asking if she could still love me. The next day at school, I gave it to her—then ran off to class. All day I was a wreck, wondering how she would react.

After school, I was on my way to my part-time job when I passed a convenience store and saw Jodi inside, buying a soda. She saw me walking by and ran out, shouting, "Yes! *Of course* I still love you!" I was ecstatic.

BRIGHT FUTURE

Jodi and I have been together for two and a half years now, and we're incredibly in love. Looking back, I can't believe I spent so much time denying my true emotions! I'm so much happier now that I'm being honest about who I am. We'd eventually like to get married and raise a family. But before that can happen, the world needs to accept our kind of relationship. It doesn't seem likely now, but I believe we'll have the chance—someday.

why i broke up with you

In a letter to his ex, Alex, 21, explains why he had to end it. Read on to avoid learning her lesson the hard way.

HEY,

When we met, you were the most confident girl—you always had something smart or funny and sarcastic to say. You pushed my buttons in a *good* way. I loved being with you, so I asked you out. And at first, dating you was amazing—I felt like I'd met my match. But after about a month, it all started to change.

YOU DIDN'T SPEAK UP

The first thing I noticed was how you stopped making your own decisions—everything was left up to me, which was weird. It was like you had lost your personality overnight. Seriously, every time I asked you what restaurant we should eat at or what movie you wanted to see, you'd just shrug your shoulders and say that you didn't care. Then when I'd go ahead and make the decision for the both of us, you'd start sulking, as if it wasn't what you had wanted. Constantly having to deal with your childish pouting really got on my nerves because there wasn't anything I could do about it. There was no way for me to know what you were thinking unless you had told me—I'm not a mind reader. If you had just been more straightforward and said what would have made you happy, I would have done it for you—but you never gave me that chance.

YOU DIDN'T TRUST ME

The next thing I knew, I started getting tons of phone calls from you—like, eight or nine a day. You didn't have anything to talk about, so it felt like you were just checking up on me. I remember one day when I was at my job, you called a few times. I didn't pick up because I had work to do, but that night you flipped out and demanded to know what had been going on that was more important than our relationship. If *that*

> **66 There was no way for me to know what you were thinking. 99**

wasn't crazy enough, just a few days later you hinted that I might be hooking up with some female friends. Anyone who knows me knows I've never thought about doing *anything* with them besides being their friend— so that was ridiculous. I cared about you and trusted you, but you didn't trust me, and that hurt. I was always faithful because I liked you and respected you, but you never seemed to respect my right to have a life outside of us. I need a girl who will trust me as much as

I trust her. Otherwise, there's nothing to build a relationship on.

YOU OVERANALYZED

I'm only human, so sometimes when I say things, they come out wrong. But whenever I said something that would upset you, you'd never talk to me about it—you'd stew over it for days until you got so upset about what I "meant" that you'd explode in a full-blown tantrum. It got to a point where you were analyzing everything I did or said. I can remember times where I didn't even say anything to you, and you'd decide I was angry or trying to hurt you. And because you thought about it for so long before mentioning it to me, it was impossible to make you believe anything else. If you'd asked me what I meant at the time or told me that you were upset, I would have been able to explain—or apologize if I needed to. But you were constantly picking me apart—and pretty soon it just wasn't fun to be around you anymore.

I WISH YOU LUCK

I've heard you're with a new guy now—and that things aren't going well. I guess you didn't learn much from me, but I hope someday you do—deep down I know you're still the fun girl you were when we first met. One day you'll be a great girlfriend to some guy if you can learn to relax a little. It's just too late for that guy to be *me*.

Take care,
Alex

one of
the boys

Do guys see you as a friend but never as a *girl*friend? That was 19-year-old Katie's problem—until she met her match.

growing up I loved sports and was the only girl in all my neighborhood football games. Being so athletic made me popular with the guys, which I loved. Like whenever I'd walk into class, I'd say, "Did anyone see the game last night?" and they'd all gather around. But as I got older and wanted to be more than just friends, things began to backfire.

SINGLED OUT

The first week of my freshman year in high school, I noticed this hot guy, Nick, in my gym class. He was tall with dark hair—not to mention a great athlete. So finally, after class one October day, I decided to make a move. Since I'm an Oakland A's fan and he was wearing a San Francisco Giants hat, I went up to him. "Wrong side of the Bay Area," I teased. "What do *you* know about the Giants?" he shot back. "I know the A's are better," I replied. Even though we were arguing, I was just excited to be talking to him!

95

A couple weeks later, Nick and I traded numbers, and for the next few months, we spoke almost every night about our shared love: baseball. I hoped that he'd ask me out—but he never did. Then finally one night in July, nine months after our first conversation, I was at home when an IM popped up from Nick: "Do you want to be my girlfriend?" was all it said. I'd started to wonder if Nick would *ever* see me that way. So I was so relieved and happy that he did! We started going everywhere together, from movies to A's games.

But a month after that, on my way back from a softball tournament in Hawaii, Nick paged me to tell me to check my IM as soon as I got home. "I thought about it while you were gone," he'd written, "and I can't be with you. We spend too much time together. It's great that we can talk baseball, but it's too much with dating." I was completely shocked; I thought Nick *liked* that I could relate to him and we could do everything together. I just wrote, "OK," before I started to cry.

Nick wasn't the only guy to break my heart. Every time I liked someone, I'd use my sports knowledge to get close to him—and he'd end up writing me off as "one of the guys." Like sophomore year, I overheard Danny, who I had a crush on, say to the girl *he* evidently liked, "Don't worry, that's just Katie—we talk baseball." And then junior year, my friend A.J., who I thought was starting to like me, ended up getting back with his ex and telling me, "I just like chilling with you as friends. I mean, we like the same *teams*!" I lost my confidence; I thought I'd *never* find a guy who'd want to date me.

GREAT CATCH

About a year ago, I moved to Arizona for college and got a job at a nearby Foot Locker. I'd watch sports on the overhead TVs with the guys I worked with, so I was sure they only considered me a friend, just like in high school. Even so, I couldn't ignore my growing feelings for one of them, Darin. So in April, I invited him to a Diamondbacks game, since he's a baseball fanatic too. He said yes—and before long we were actually dating, hanging out four or five nights a week!

A few months into our relationship, Darin and I were watching *SportsCenter*, and I was wearing my silver hoop earrings that have a little bat, ball, and glove dangling from them. Suddenly he turned to me and said out of the blue, "You don't know how happy it makes me to see that earring." But he didn't know how happy it made *me* to know that there are guys out there who appreciate having common interests with a girl. Thank God I never compromised my passion for a few high school relationships. Because now I know that there will be even *more* passion in my future.

the other woman

Jennifer, 20, dated a guy she really liked—even though she knew he had a girlfriend. What happens when you fall in love with a cheater?

the second week of my sophomore year in college, my sorority had a mixer at a frat house, where I immediately noticed this tall guy with dark hair and dimples. We made eye contact a few times before he waved me over so we could talk. His name was Mike* and he was my year. He was funny and flirty—and soon he was feeding me an ice-cream pop! As we laughed at the mess we were making, I thought, I could date him.

After talking the whole night, Mike grabbed my hand and kissed me. Even though I had butterflies, I also felt really comfortable, like I'd known him forever. Then the next evening Mike called to invite me to his frat to hang out—I was *so* excited! The whole night he kept his arm around me, like he was so proud to be by my side. Then the next night we hung out *again*, and I was *sure* we were going to be a long-term thing—so we had sex.

A week later, I was walking on campus and ran into a guy I know from Mike's hometown. When I told him

Name has been changed.

that I was dating Mike, he just looked at me and asked, "Doesn't he already have a girlfriend?" I got so confused. "She's your year," he continued, sounding sure that he was right. Suddenly I felt like I'd been kicked in the stomach, and I ran home and called Mike. "Is there something you want to tell me?" I demanded. "No," he said, surprised, adding, "Why don't I call you later—when you stop acting weird?" So I just said, "Why don't you call when you don't have a *girlfriend*?"

MAJOR DECEPTION

Mike was silent. "How did you find out?" he finally asked. "Why?!" I yelled back. But "I'm sorry," was all he said. I was so mad I told him never to call me again.

> **66 He was acting like he didn't even *know* me. 99**

But at 10 p.m. the next night, my phone rang, and it was Mike. "What are you doing?" he asked. "Um, I don't know," I said, baffled but a little intrigued. "Okay, I'll call you later," he said. And he did. Mike began calling every night, and I started to wonder if maybe he'd rather be with me than his girlfriend. I figured that at the very least it meant we had something special—why else would he risk his relationship for us? So about a month later, when Mike's girlfriend was away, I let him come over. I still liked him so much that we had sex again (I couldn't help it!). After that we'd see each other three nights a week—whenever he wasn't with her.

But then a month later, on November 20, I walked into a party and I saw Mike—kissing his girlfriend! It was the first time I'd seen her, and I wanted to cry. He was focused on her like she was the only one there—and that's how he usually made *me* feel! He was also acting like he didn't even *know* me. So when she wasn't looking, I mouthed, "It's over," and left.

But Mike made it hard for me to actually end things! Like a few weeks later, he stopped by with egg rolls (my favorite) just to make me smile. I know it sounds lame, but it won me back—no guy had ever done something just to make me happy like that before.

After winter break, Mike and I picked back up. A few times I tried to ask him why he didn't just break up with his girlfriend, but he'd say, "I'm just not ready." Yes, it was hard seeing them together—it made me feel guilty that she was oblivious. But staying with Mike gave me an odd sense of security, knowing nothing could hurt more than when I first found out about his girlfriend.

REALITY CHECK

Two nights before school ended—eight months after I'd met Mike—I was at a party when my friend JT asked, "Are you gonna *stay* with him?!" I'd been asked that 100 times before, but I knew it was time to confront it: Mike and I weren't going anywhere, and I needed summer break to get over him. So later that night, when Mike sat down next to me, I blurted out, "We should stop."

Five months later, I'm happy to say that I have a new boyfriend. Though Mike and I don't hook up anymore, we talk almost every day. I still think he's great, but I realize I deserve a guy who wants only *one* girl—me.

summer romance

Think long-term relationships are the only ones that are truly meaningful? Not always. Liz, 16, dated a guy for just a few weeks— but he changed her life forever.

my sophomore year of high school, I had a crush on Darin, a junior in my Diplomacy Club. He had these amazing dark eyes and wore wire-rimmed glasses that made him look so handsome. We were friendly, and sometimes he'd even call me after school to talk about the club, but I never considered pursuing him. You see, I was more of an artsy girl, and Darin hung out with the smart crowd. Plus, my ex-boyfriend—who wasn't *nearly* as smart and funny as Darin—had cheated on me, so I figured if I wasn't good enough for *him*, a guy like Darin would never give me the time of day.

TAKING A CHANCE

When the school year ended, I wanted to get away from everything I knew and go on an adventure. So on July 1, I flew from Massachusetts, where I live, to Montana for a month-long backpacking trip with 12 kids I'd never met before. I was nervous but also excited to spend time with a group of people who knew nothing about what I was like at school or who I was friends with—there weren't any expectations, so I could act how I wanted.

As soon as I got to the campsite, I immediately noticed this tall guy with curly blond hair and bright blue eyes named Danny who was from California. And once we started to talk, I realized he wasn't just cute—he also had the same smart, offbeat sense of humor as Darin!

About five days into our trip, a bunch of us went down to the stream to wash our dishes. "Will you clean the pot?" I asked Danny. "What will you give me if I do?" he asked teasingly. Well, usually I would have been too insecure to flirt with a guy as funny and confident as Danny, but in the split second before I answered, I realized Danny had no way of knowing that about me—and this was my moment to take a chance.

> **66 I just wanted to tell him how I felt. 99**

Suddenly I felt free. "I'll love you forever," I said with a smile. "Really?" he asked. "No!" I replied, laughing.

MAKING A MOVE

For the next two weeks, I kept flirting with Danny. One night the group decided to sleep outside of our tents, and I set up my sleeping bag right next to his! But for whatever reason, nothing happened. Since my "fresh start" didn't seem to be working, I began to wonder if I'd *ever* be the kind of girl a great guy like this would like. I wanted some time alone to think and write in my journal, so one evening I headed to a nearby hill. On my way, I bumped into Danny. We'd never really been alone, so I thought I should take the opportunity to see if there could be anything between us—and I asked him to come along.

When we got to the hill, we laid down on our backs. I'd gone this far, and I just wanted to tell him how I felt: "I'm glad I'm not out here alone," I whispered. "Me too," he said—and he leaned over and kissed me! Every night after that, the two of us went to the hill together.

Since Danny and I lived so far apart, we agreed that our relationship would end with the backpacking trip. But we still got close. One night I even opened up about my cheating ex and Darin. "That's horrible," he said. "You deserve better—maybe Darin will ask you out." I just laughed. I didn't think that would ever happen.

A week later, Danny and I said goodbye at the airport. As I watched him walk away, I knew I was going to miss him terribly. But I was grateful that we'd had our time together: I took a chance with Danny, and it paid off. Now I knew that I could be the kind of girl I wanted to be—and someone as great as Danny would like me for it.

FINDING TRUE LOVE

Over the next month I missed Danny, but I also couldn't stop thinking about what he'd said about Darin. I mean, what if Darin might like me? So about a month later, right before school started, I got up the courage to call Darin and invite him over. I couldn't believe he said yes!

A few nights later, Darin and I were lying together on my dock, looking up at the stars. After a long pause, he asked, "Liz, do you like me?" I was so nervous that I started to shake, but I managed to say, "Yes." "Good," he said, "because I like you too." Then he kissed my hand.

Darin and I have been together for seven months, and we're totally in love. He's my best friend, and I can't imagine ever being with anyone else, but even so, I'll never forget Danny. If it wasn't for him, I never would have found the confidence to go after a guy like Darin.

i'm a player

Dani, 19, always flirted with a million guys. But there was a deeper problem—one that she couldn't ignore.

a s a child I dreamed of one day having a fairy-tale romance with an amazing guy. But when I started dating in ninth grade, I quickly discovered that as soon as a guy told me he liked me, I stopped wanting him. Once I knew his true feelings, he seemed vulnerable to me, which made him look weak—and that was a huge turnoff. So all through high school, I flirted like crazy with guys I thought were cute, always looking for that fairy-tale romance. But after we'd hook up and I *knew* he wanted me, I'd almost always walk away. I didn't do it to hurt anyone, but I guess I liked the challenge of getting a guy to notice me—and feeling that sense of control. I did still want to have an amazing relationship, but I really needed to find a guy who was as strong and confident as I was. I figured that would happen when I went away to college.

NEW BEGINNING

In September 2004 I started freshman year at the University of Miami. On the first night I was sitting in

107

the lobby of my dorm when I locked eyes with a hot guy across the room. I smiled, and he came over to sit next to me on the couch. "Hey, I'm Travis," he said. "Dani," I replied. We talked for about 20 minutes, and I was excited that this might be the confident guy I needed.

After that night, Travis and I talked online almost every day and realized we had a lot in common, especially our tastes in music. I was starting to really like him, but we didn't hang out with each other that much because he began pledging a fraternity and I met a different group of friends. Then that November, two months after we had met, Travis finally made a move: "You're so hot, you have the body of a goddess," he wrote to me one night.

> ❝ I liked the challenge of getting a guy to notice me. ❞

It was really forward—but I was totally flattered. I quickly typed back, "What are you doing? I need a study break. Want to come over?" He replied, "Sorry, I've got too much work." I was stunned! I knew he liked me, so I figured he was too scared to follow through. Maybe he *wasn't* as confident as I had thought.

ONGOING CYCLE

Travis kept flirting over the next few months. I liked that he always told me I was cute and sexy, but he never seemed to have the nerve to take things further. That made me stop thinking of him as a possible boyfriend, but I was still interested in him—as a challenge. Now I wanted to get him to prove that I *could*—and so the games started. Whenever he'd e-mail or IM me, instead of responding right away, I'd ignore him, so he'd get insecure and call me to make sure everything was okay between us. Trying to keep him guessing about what I was thinking made me feel more in control of our situation.

Then one Wednesday night in May 2005, I was studying for my last final exam in the library and noticed Travis sitting a few desks away. I decided to make my move. "I'm not wearing any panties," I wrote to him in a text message. He glanced in my direction, then wrote, "Scandalous, can I verify?" My plan worked: He was finally ready to do something about our long, drawn-out flirtation. Excited and feeling victorious, I left the library with Travis, and we went back to my room. We immediately started making out. "Can we say this was special?" Travis asked when we were done hooking up. I didn't say a word—because now that I'd been with Travis, I didn't want him anymore. I just couldn't see myself dating a guy who was so afraid to go after what he wanted. "You should leave," I abruptly told him. Looking confused and hurt, Travis replied, "Sure . . . I'll call you." Then he got dressed and left.

GAME OVER

The next afternoon I went home for the summer. I felt bad about how things ended with Travis—and it made me wonder if my expectations about guys were realistic. Then the following fall I finally met an amazing, confident guy, and we've been dating for three months. I'm not sure why, but knowing he likes me *isn't* a turnoff—it makes me like him more.

virginity lost

Anna, 18, though all her friends were much more sexually experienced than she was— so she decided to do something about it.

back in high school, I was always known as outgoing and wild—and I loved it. It was an ego boost to be seen as the confident girl who could talk to any guy—the one people wanted to party with. The only problem was that I constantly felt like I was living a lie: Even though everyone thought I was this crazy, fun girl, the truth was, I'd never even had sex. My freshman-year boyfriend hadn't felt ready to sleep with me, and then for the rest of high school, I never really had another serious boyfriend. I was always afraid that people would find out the truth, and I'd suddenly lose my cool reputation.

On my first night of college in September 2001, a bunch of girls got together in someone's room. The conversation quickly turned to sex—and everyone began talking about their first time. Mortified that I didn't have a story to share, I slipped out the door. All right, I thought, I'm

111

going to lose my virginity. I was *not* about to let the fact that I'd never had sex turn me into a loser.

BIG IDEA

I made a plan: I'd go to as many parties as possible in search of a cute, nice guy for a one-night stand. I didn't need a boyfriend—there would be plenty of time for that. I just needed someone fun to do the "deed" with.

I was going to about five parties a week, when one Saturday night in October I ended up at this frat party with some friends. A few minutes after getting there, I noticed a cute guy staring at me and smiling. Suddenly he walked over. "Hi, I'm Carlo," he said. Oh my God, I thought to myself, this could be my perfect chance!

> **66 Right away I started flirting like mad, touching his arm and laughing at everything. 99**

Right away I started flirting like mad, touching his arm and laughing at everything. Finally, after talking for about an hour, Carlo reached out and brushed my hair away from my face. Then he slowly leaned in and kissed me. I was so excited—my plan was falling into place! When my friends and I left a half hour later, I gave Carlo my number and told him to *definitely* call.

SUDDEN SEDUCTION

Carlo called the next day, and we decided to see a movie that Thursday. That's it, I thought, I'm not letting our date end without having sex! When Thursday arrived, Carlo picked me up and I hopped into his car. All of a sudden I felt so nervous. But I'd made an important pact with myself—and I wasn't going to break it.

At the movies, Carlo and I held hands and I began to feel calmer. It seemed like he was into me, so maybe it would be easy (even fun!) to go through with my plan. As soon as the film ended, I told Carlo I wanted to see his place. He looked a bit surprised, but smiled and said

> **66 I was nervous—but also relieved it was finally happening. 99**

okay. Once we got there I sat on the couch next to him. Go ahead, I coaxed myself—and I leaned in to kiss his neck.

Before I knew it we were in Carlo's room, making out. "This will be my first time—but it's not a big deal," I blurted out. "Uh, okay," he said, shocked. I figured he was just confused about why I would want to lose my virginity on a random night like this. "So you might bleed?" he asked. He went into the bathroom and came back with a towel and a condom. I took off my shirt—then he pulled off my pants and yanked off his clothes. I was nervous again—but also relieved it was *finally* happening. Carlo lay on top of me, and I felt some pressure and pain. But then just moments later, it was over. That's it? I thought, disappointed. *That* won't make a great story. I didn't know what else to say or do, so I sat up and started to get dressed—Carlo was silent. "Well… bye?" I mumbled. "Later," was all he said.

TOTAL LETDOWN

I hurried back to my dorm's common room, where a group of girls was eating pizza. "You're not gonna believe what I did…" I started, so happy I finally had a sex story. But when I finished, they seemed *horrified*. "*Really*?!" one girl said. "I can't believe you had random sex." Someone else added: "I couldn't do that—I'm waiting for the perfect guy." Then *another* girl agreed! Suddenly it hit me: I'd assumed I was the only virgin—but I wasn't! I was just the only one who was obsessed with my sexual status. What I'd done with Carlo didn't make me cool—it made me seem *desperate*.

> **❝ I'd assumed I was the only virgin—but I wasn't! I was just the only one who was obsessed with my sexual status. ❞**

Looking back four years later, I wish I'd made a different decision that night. Now I've fallen for a great guy and I see that sex is something you enjoy most with a person you love. *I* just had to learn the hard way.

the freeloader

Nicole, 18, fell in love with a guy who was broke. But did her decision to spoil him destroy their relationship?

bryan and I met at a party in January 2000 at Villanova University, where he was a junior and I was a freshman. I thought he was cute, so I started trying to run into him between classes. In April I finally got up the nerve to ask Bryan out— luckily he said yes! We went to T.G.I. Friday's, and our date lasted for hours. We were so absorbed in our conversation that I didn't want it to end. When the check finally came, he glanced at it—but never picked it up. I waited a few minutes, thinking he might still go for it. He didn't—so I grabbed it and said, "I invited *you*, so *I'll* pay." He just said, "Thanks." I felt hurt that he didn't treat me—like he thought of it as a friendly dinner, not a *real* date. But I figured if I paid, I might impress him with the fact that I could take care of him, and he'd want to see me again.

BIG SPENDER

For the next two months, Bryan and I hung out almost every single day and were totally falling in love. In June, he moved into a new apartment, and when I

117

stopped by to see it, I was appalled! The building was crumbling and paint was peeling off the walls. Bryan saw my horror and turned red. "It's all I can afford," he said. "I'll help you make it look nice," I told him. I had a job, so it was no big deal to me financially—and I really wanted to make him happy. So I brought him area rugs and pictures for the walls. He was surprised when I gave him these things but also very thankful. Plus, he showed that he loved me in other ways, like with flowers and cute cards.

> **66 I felt he should have been more grateful for all the things I'd done. 99**

In January 2001, Bryan and I had been going out for eight months, and I wanted to do something great for his birthday—so I got him a $200 PlayStation 2. When I went to his place and gave it to him, he just muttered, "Wow, thanks." He *seemed* happy, but not nearly as happy as I was expecting. I was crushed—it was like he took for granted that I'd buy him expensive gifts!

MAJOR REJECTION

That May, Bryan was graduating, and again I wanted to get him an even bigger gift—one that would remind him of me and the place where we met. So I saved for months and bought him a $400 class ring. I was so excited to see his reaction when I handed it to him—but his face tensed up. "I don't want this," he said. "Why not?" I asked. "I *never* liked this school," he snapped. I was shocked! He'd told me that he didn't

118

love school, but I had no idea he *hated* it. All I could think about was that I'd worked so hard to buy this gift, and he was refusing it—it felt like he was refusing *me*! "If you don't want it, fine!" I screamed. Then I grabbed the ring and left.

Bryan called later that day, but I didn't pick up. He phoned every day for a week and finally showed up at my door. I *did* miss him, so I let him in to talk. "I love *you*," he explained. "It's the *school* I want to forget." I still felt he should have been more grateful—not just for the ring, but for all the things I'd done. I'd spent more than $5,000 on him, which was almost all my savings! But I still loved him, so I said, "Let's just forget it."

COSTLY ENDING

In the fall, Bryan got a job. He was earning money and started paying for our dates. I thought I'd be happy to finally be the one getting treated, but instead I hated that he didn't need me to take care of him anymore. The next summer, I told him we had to break up. He was crushed, but I said, "We're different people now."

Looking back, I see what a big mistake I made. It was wrong for me to use money to keep Bryan dependent on me and to stay in control of the relationship. I loved the power—and couldn't deal when that changed. But I guess for love to last, *no one* can have the upper hand.

love
letters

Emily, 17, couldn't believe it when her boyfriend, Kevin, then 18, joined the Army— and was later sent to the Middle East. But notes like these kept their love strong.

8/27/02

Dear Emily: Good Morning, Beautiful! It's our two-year anniversary, and I want you to know how lucky I feel. Honestly, I don't think I could have made it through basic training and the start of active duty without you motivating me. Now that you're going to college, it's my turn to be supportive of you.

9/24/02

Kevin, do you think you could ever fall out of love with me? I know you're probably rolling your eyes—but I keep thinking I have to make my letters creative and interesting to keep your attention. But I'm not that creative and I don't always have interesting things to say. It's hard to do special things for you from so far away. I just don't want to become boring or ordinary to you.

10/08/02

Hey, Princess, you know I still love you and always will
no matter what. Your letters are perfect—I read them
all the time. I want to see you ASAP. Hang on. I should
be home in six months!

10/21/02

Kevin, I just want to pick up the phone and call you,
but I can't. And that absolutely blows monkey balls! I
miss you so much, but you know what? The other night
I was with the girls at this party and some guy asked
me out. I thought it was a great sign because I'm
meeting all these new people at school, and all I want
to do is be with you.

11/08/02

Em, what the hell, somebody asked you out? Why did
he think you were available? I am trusting you and will
always trust you. But please don't give me any reason
to think that you are getting lonely and need somebody
besides me.
P.S. Didn't he see the promise ring on your finger?

11/20/02

Dear Kevin: I often imagine us lying in the
grass together looking up at the sky, just talking
and laughing. We're not really saying anything, just
things like the famous people we want to meet and
our dreams and stories. I know it sounds petty, but
I've always pictured it as the "perfect relationship"
because I can be with you and just chill. I used to
be afraid that you would never be like this, but
I feel like you've become a lot more open lately.

And I love it!
P.S. No one is a threat to you!

1/07/03

Well Em, things are starting to unfold. Two of our battleships were deployed, and Saudi Arabia said we could fight out of their air-force bases. So I dunno. . . . But by the time you get this letter, things will probably be out in the open and all news will be bad news.

2/6/03

Dear Kev: So it sounds like we're definitely going to war. All I can think in response to this is, F*** war! and f*** Iraq! I can't explain how scared I am. I've prayed to God—begged him to keep you safe and bring you home on time in April. But I still can't stop my mind from thinking about the "what ifs." What if you don't come home? I'd die.

3/29/03

Well, Em, now that we're at war, I won't be coming home anytime soon. But the good news is, after nine days of fighting, we were ambushed only two times and lost just one vehicle. Thanks to God listening to your (and everyone's) prayers, nobody was even injured. Em, please don't worry about me. Focus on your schoolwork. I'll be okay.

4/7/03

Dear Kevin: Truthfully, I feel like the worst girlfriend because I don't know what to do for you. People keep asking what they can send you, and I don't know. I write to you every chance I get, but I want you to know that there isn't a moment that I'm not sending you my love. I hope that you can still feel it. Stay strong, Kev, I love you!

5/30/03

Princess, it looks like my unit is going into Fallujah on June 5. I don't know what to say. The worst-case scenario is that I'll be home in August. Honestly, I don't know what to write, but please have patience. The way I look at it is it means more money for us—and I do mean *us*. Being over here makes me realize how much I need you. I love you, Em, and I swear I am coming home to you.